Jumbo Crochet

by Lisa Gentry

Table of Contents

Leisure Arts Inc. • Maumellle, Arkansas

THROW

Finished Size:
50" x 45" (127 cm x 114.5 cm)
(slightly stretched)

SHOPPING LIST

Yarn (Jumbo Weight)

[10 ounces, 29 yards
(283 grams, 26 meters) per skein]:

- ☐ 14 skeins

Crochet Hook

- ☐ Size Q (15 mm)
  or size needed for gauge

Additional Supplies

- ☐ Yarn needle

GAUGE INFORMATION

In extended slip st pattern,
4 sts = 5" (12.5 cm);
4 rows = 5½" (14 cm)

STITCH GUIDE

EXTENDED SLIP STITCH ***(abbreviated ex slip st)***

YO, insert hook in st indicated, YO and pull loop through st **and** through both loops on hook.

Note: Throw is worked from side-to-side.

Ch 41.

Row 1 (Right side)**:** Work ex slip st in second ch from hook and in each ch across: 40 ex slip sts.

Note: Loop a short piece of yarn around any stitch to mark Row 1 as **right** side.

Rows 2-32: Ch 1, turn; work ex slip st in **Back Loop Only** of each st across ***(Fig. 7, page 32)***.

Row 33: Ch 2 **(counts as first hdc)**, turn; hdc in both loops of next st and in each st across; finish off.

PILLOW

Finished Size: 22" (56 cm) square

SHOPPING LIST

Yarn (Jumbo Weight) JUMBO 7

[5 ounces, 55 yards
(141 grams, 50 meters) per skein]:

- ☐ 6 skeins

Crochet Hook

- ☐ Size Q (15 mm)
  or size needed for gauge

Additional Supplies

- ☐ 24" (61 cm) Square pillow insert
- ☐ Yarn needle

GAUGE INFORMATION

In pattern, 6 sts = 5" (12.75 cm)
and Rows 1-4 = 4" (10 cm)

STITCH GUIDE

PUFF ST (uses one sc)

Insert hook in sc indicated, YO and pull up a loop (2 loops on hook), ★ YO, insert hook in **same** st, YO and pull up a loop; repeat from ★ 2 times **more**, YO and draw through all 8 loops on hook.

FRONT

Ch 28.

Row 1 (Right side)**:** Hdc in second ch from hook and in each ch across: 27 hdc.

Note: Loop a short piece of yarn around any stitch to mark Row 1 as **right** side.

Row 2: Ch 1, turn; sc in horizontal bar of each hdc across ***(Fig. A)***.

Fig. A

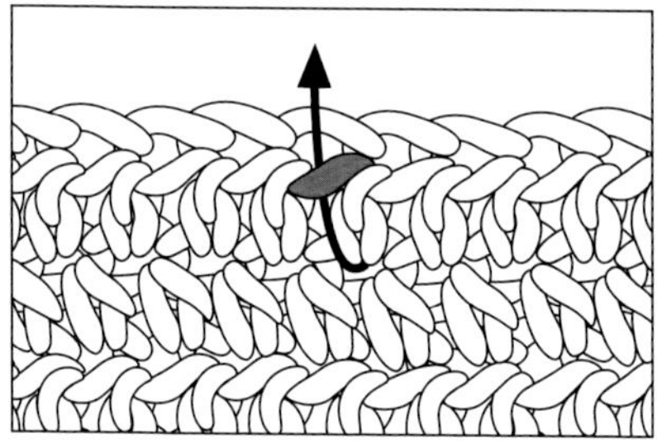

Row 3: Ch 1, turn; sc in both loops of each sc across.

Row 4: Ch 1, turn; hdc in first 2 sc, work Puff St in next sc, ★ ch 1, skip next sc, work Puff St in next sc; repeat from ★ across to last 2 sc, hdc in last 2 hdc: 12 Puff Sts, 4 hdc and 11 ch-1 sps.

Row 5: Ch 1, turn; hdc in each first 2 hdc and in next Puff St, (hdc in next ch-1 sp and in next Puff St) across to last 2 hdc, hdc in last 2 hdc: 27 hdc.

Rows 6-23: Repeat Rows 2-5, 4 times; then repeat Rows 2 and 3 once **more**.

Finish off.

BACK

Work same as Front, but do **not** finish off at end of Row 23.

ASSEMBLY

Ch 1, turn; placing **wrong** side of Back against **wrong** side of Front, having sts of Row 23 matching and working through **both** loops on **both** pieces, work 3 sc in first sc, sc in each st across to last st, 3 sc in last sc; working in end of rows through **both** pieces, work 25 sc evenly spaced across; working in free loops of beginning ch ***(Fig. 6, page 32)*** on **both** pieces, work 3 sc in first ch, sc in next 25 chs, 3 sc in next ch, insert pillow insert; working in end of rows through **both** pieces, work 25 sc evenly spaced across; join with slip st to first sc, finish off.

SHAWL

 **EASY**

Finished Size: 66" wide x 16½" deep
(167.5 cm x 42 cm)

SHOPPING LIST

Yarn (Jumbo Weight)

[10.5 ounces, 64 yards
(300 grams, 58 meters) per skein]:

- ☐ 4 skeins

Crochet Hook

- ☐ Size Q (15 mm)
  or size needed for gauge

Additional Supplies

- ☐ Yarn needle

GAUGE INFORMATION

In pattern,
7¾ sts and 7¼ rows = 4" (10 cm)

Note: Shawl is worked from side-to-side. Work slip sts **loose** enough to be able to insert your hook on the next row.

INCREASING SECTION

Foundation Row (Right side)**:** Ch 2, (slip st, ch 1, slip st) in second ch from hook: 3 sts.

Note: Loop a short piece of yarn around any stitch to mark Foundation Row as **right** side.

Row 1: Ch 1, turn; slip st in Back Loop Only of each st across ***(Fig. 7, page 32)***: 3 slip sts.

Row 2 (Increase row)**:** Ch 2, turn; slip st in second ch from hook and in Back Loop Only of each st across: 4 slip sts.

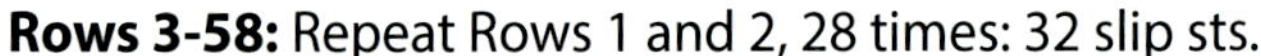

Rows 3-58: Repeat Rows 1 and 2, 28 times: 32 slip sts.

DECREASING SECTION

Row 1: Ch 1, turn; slip st in Back Loop Only of each st across: 32 slip sts.

Row 2 (Decrease row)**:** Ch 1, turn; skip first slip st, slip st in Back Loop Only of each st across: 31 slip sts.

Rows 3-58: Repeat Rows 1 and 2, 28 times: 3 slip sts.

Next Row: Ch 1, turn; skip first slip st, slip st in Back Loops Only of last 2 slip sts: 2 slip sts.

Last Row: Ch 1, turn; skip first slip st, slip st in Back Loop Only of last slip st; finish off.

COWL

EASY

Finished Size: 28" wide x 9½" long
(71 cm x 24 cm)
Across neck edge: 19" (48.5 cm)

SHOPPING LIST

Yarn (Jumbo Weight) JUMBO 7

[10.5 ounces, 64 yards
(300 grams, 48 meters) per skein**]**:

- ☐ Light Grey - 2 skeins
- ☐ Purple - 1 skein

Crochet Hook

- ☐ Size Q (15 mm)
  or size needed for gauge

Additional Supplies

- ☐ Yarn needle

GAUGE INFORMATION

In pattern,
7 sts and 8 rows = 4" (10 cm)

Note: Cowl is worked from side-to-side. Work slip sts **loose** enough to be able to insert your hook on the next row.

With Light Grey and leaving a 40" (101.5 cm) length, ch 20.

Foundation Row (Right side)**:** Slip st in top loop of second ch from hook and each ch across ***(Fig. 5, page 32)***: 19 slip sts.

Note: Loop a short piece of yarn around any stitch to mark Foundation Row as **right** side.

Row 1: Ch 1, turn; slip st in Back Loop Only of each slip st across ***(Fig. 7, page 32)***.

Row 2: Ch 1, turn; slip st in Front Loop Only of each slip st across ***(Fig. 7, page 32)***.

Rows 3-9: Repeat Rows 1 and 2, 3 times; then repeat Row 1 once **more**, at end of Row 9, finish off.

Row 11: With **right** side facing, join Purple with slip st in Back Loop Only of first slip st ***(Fig. 2, page 30)***; slip st in Back Loop Only of each slip st across.

Row 12: Ch 1, turn; slip st in Front Loop Only of each slip st across; finish off.

Row 13: With **right** side facing, join Light Grey with slip st in Back Loop Only of first slip st; slip st in Back Loops Only of each slip st across.

Row 14: Ch 1, turn; slip st in Front Loop Only of each slip st across.

Row 15: Ch 1, turn; slip st in Back Loop Only of each slip st across.

Rows 16-59: Repeat Rows 14 and 15, 22 times.

Do **not** finish off.

Neck Edging: Ch 1, work 30 slip sts evenly spaced across end of rows; finish off.

With **right** side facing and working in free loops of beginning ch ***(Fig. 6, page 32)***, insert hook in first ch, YO with beginning end and pull up a loop; slip st in each free loop across; finish off.

With Purple, make two, 3½" (9 cm) pom-poms ***(Figs. 8a-c, page 33)***, using a 60" (152.5 cm) length of yarn to wrap; do **not** cut long ends.

Beginning at neck edge, weave end from pom-pom down through sts on short edge for approximately 7" (18 cm), and secure end on wrong side. Repeat on opposite side.

HAT

EASY

Finished Size:
22" (56 cm) circumference;
9" (23 cm) deep (without pom-pom)

SHOPPING LIST

Yarn (Jumbo Weight) JUMBO 7

[10.5 ounces, 64 yards
(300 grams, 58 meters) per skein**]**:

- ☐ Light Grey - 2 skeins
- ☐ Purple - 1 skein

Crochet Hook

- ☐ Size Q (15 mm)
  or size needed for gauge

Additional Supplies

- ☐ Yarn needle

GAUGE INFORMATION

In Waistcoat pattern,
4½ sts and 7 rows/rnds = 4" (10 cm)

STITCH GUIDE

WAISTCOAT STITCH *(abbreviated WCst)*

A Waistcoat stitch is worked like a single crochet EXCEPT that the hook is inserted between the two leaning vertical strands that form a "V" on the front of the stitch, instead of under the top 2 loops. Insert hook between the "legs" of the next st ***(Fig. A)***, YO and pull up a loop, YO and draw through both loops on hook.

Fig. A

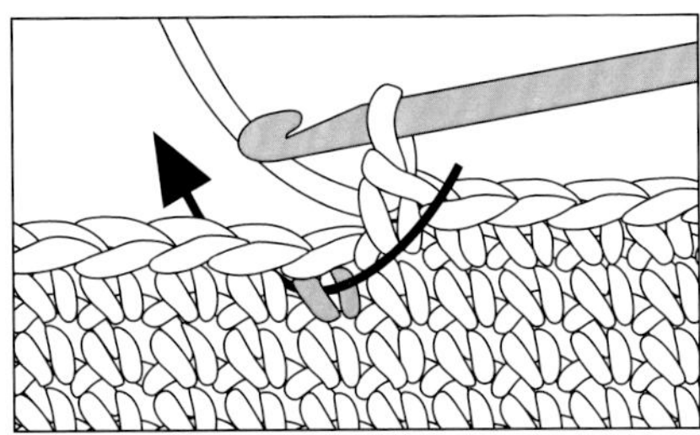

BODY

Rnd 1 (Right side)**:** With Light Grey, make an adjustable ring to form a ring, ch 1, 8 sc in ring ***(Figs. 4a-d, page 31)***; do **not** join, place marker to indicate the beginning of the round ***(Fig. 1, page 30)***.

Note: Loop a short piece of yarn around any stitch to mark Rnd 1 as **right** side.

Rnd 2: (WCst in next sc, 2 WCsts in next sc) around: 12 sc.

Rnd 3: (WCst in next 2 sc, 2 WCsts in next sc) around: 16 sc.

Rnd 4: (WCst in next 3 sc, 2 WCsts in next sc) around: 20 sc.

Rnd 5: (Work WCst in next 4 sc, work 2 WCsts in next sc) around: 24 sc.

Rnd 6: Work WCsts in each sc around.

Repeat Rnd 6 until Body measures 8" (20.5 cm) from beginning.

RIBBING

Rnd 1: Slip st **loosely** in Back Loop Only of each sc around *(Fig. 7, page 32)*.

Rnd 2: Slip st **loosely** in Back Loop Only of each sc around; slip st in **both** loops of next sc, finish off.

With Purple, make one pom-pom and sew to top of Hat *(Figs. 8a-c, page 33)*.

MITTENS

EASY

Finished Adult Size:
10" (25.5 cm) circumference;
8" (20.5 cm) long

SHOPPING LIST

Yarn (Jumbo Weight)

[10.5 ounces, 64 yards
(300 grams, 58 meters) per skein]:

- ☐ Light Grey - 2 skeins
- ☐ Purple - 1 skein

Crochet Hook

- ☐ Size Q (15 mm)
  or size needed for gauge

Additional Supplies

- ☐ Yarn needle

GAUGE INFORMATION

6 sc and 6 rows = 4" (10 cm)

STITCH GUIDE

SINGLE CROCHET 2 TOGETHER

(abbreviated sc2tog)

Pull up a loop in each of next 2 sts, YO and draw through all 3 loops on hook *(Fig. A)* (**counts as one sc**).

Fig. A

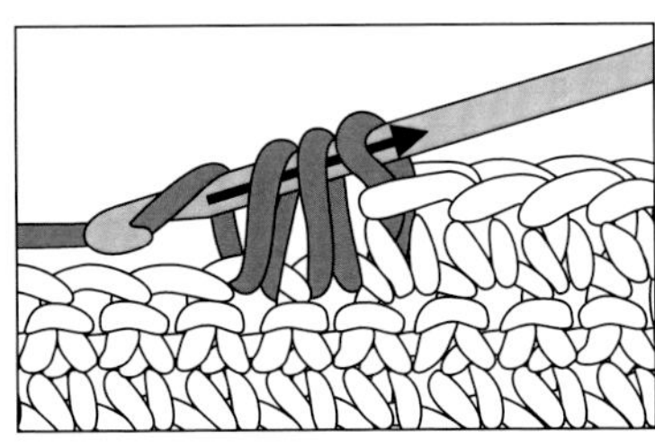

MITTEN (Make 2)

Body

Rnd 1 (Right side)**:** With Light Grey, make an adjustable ring to form a ring, ch 1, 6 sc in ring *(Figs. 4a-d, page 31)*; do **not** join, place marker to indicate the beginning of the round *(Fig. 1, page 30)*.

Note: Loop a short piece of yarn around any stitch to mark Rnd 1 as **right** side.

Rnd 2: (2 Sc in next sc, sc in next sc) around: 9 sc.

Rnd 3: (Sc in next 2 sc, 2 sc in next sc) around: 12 sc.

Rnd 4: (Sc in next 5 sc, 2 sc in next sc) twice: 14 sc.

Rnds 5-10: Sc in each sc around.

Rnd 11: Slip st in next sc, ch 3, skip next 2 sc (for thumb hole), place marker in first skipped sc for thumb placement, sc in next 11 sc; slip st in next slip st: 15 sts.

Rnd 12: Ch 1, sc in same st as slip st and in each ch and sc around; join with slip st to first sc: 15 sc.

Rnd 13: Ch 1, (sc in each of next 5 sc, sc2tog) twice; join with slip st to first sc: 13 sc.

Finish off.

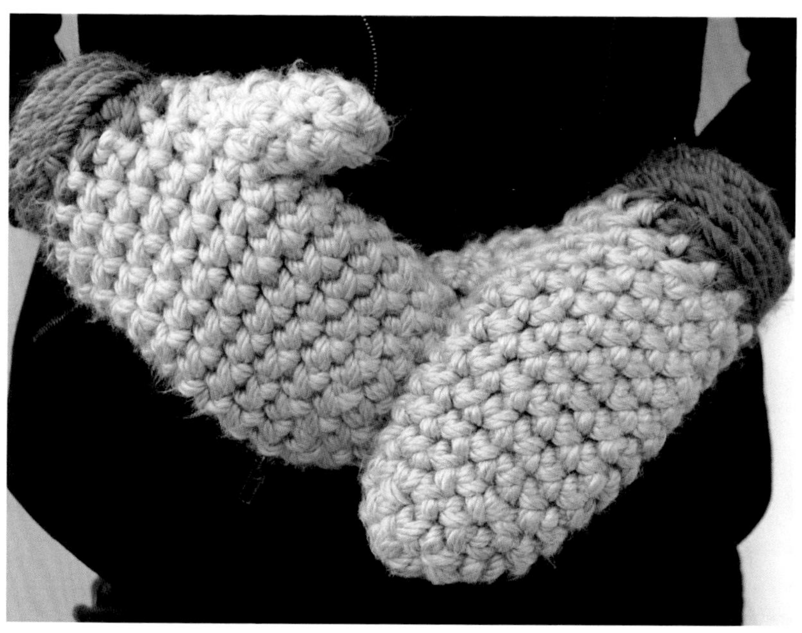

Ribbing

Rnd 1: With **right** side facing, join Purple with sc in same st as joining *(Fig.3, page 30)*; sc in each sc around; do **not** join, place marker to indicate the beginning of the round: 13 sc.

Rnds 2-5: Working in Back Loops Only *(Fig. 7, page 32)*, slip st **loosely** in each st around.

Slip st in **both** loops of next slip st, finish off.

Thumb

Rnd 1: With **right** side facing, join Light Grey with slip st in marked sc *(Fig. 2, page 30)*; ch 1, work 6 sc evenly spaced around the thumb hole; do **not** join, place marker to indicate the beginning of the round.

Rnds 2-4: Sc in each sc around.

Rnd 5: Sc2tog 3 times; finish off leaving a long end for sewing: 3 sc.

Thread yarn needle with end and weave through every stitch around the top; pull **tightly** to close and finish off.

GENERAL INSTRUCTIONS

ABBREVIATIONS

ch(s)	chain(s)
cm	centimeters
ex slip st(s)	extended slip stitch(es)
hdc	half double crochet(s)
mm	millimeters
Rnd(s)	round(s)
sc	single crochet(s)
sp(s)	space(s)
st(s)	stitch(es)
WCst(s)	Waistcoat stitch(es)
YO	yarn over

SYMBOLS & TERMS

★ — work instructions following ★ as many **more** times as indicated in addition to the first time.

( ) or [ ] — contains explanatory remarks.

colon (:) — the numbers given after a colon at the end of a row or round denotes the number of stitches or spaces you should have on that row or round.

CROCHET TERMINOLOGY		
UNITED STATES		INTERNATIONAL
slip stitch (slip st)	=	single crochet (sc)
single crochet (sc)	=	double crochet (dc)
half double crochet (hdc)	=	half treble crochet (htr)
double crochet (dc)	=	treble crochet (tr)
treble crochet (tr)	=	double treble crochet (dtr)
double treble crochet (dtr)	=	triple treble crochet (ttr)
triple treble crochet (tr tr)	=	quadruple treble crochet (qtr)
skip	=	miss

Yarn Weight Symbol & Names	LACE 0	SUPER FINE 1	FINE 2	LIGHT 3	MEDIUM 4	BULKY 5	SUPER BULKY 6	JUMBO 7
Type of Yarns in Category	Fingering, size 10 crochet thread	Sock, Fingering, Baby	Sport, Baby	DK, Light Worsted	Worsted, Afghan, Aran	Chunky, Craft, Rug	Super Bulky, Roving	Jumbo, Roving
Crochet Gauge* Ranges in Single Crochet to 4" (10 cm)	32-42 sts**	21-32 sts	16-20 sts	12-17 sts	11-14 sts	8-11 sts	6-9 sts	5 sts and fewer
Advised Hook Size Range	Steel*** 6 to 8, Regular hook B-1	B-1 to E-4	E-4 to 7	7 to I-9	I-9 to K-10½	K-10½ to M/N-13	M/N-13 to Q	Q and larger

*GUIDELINES ONLY: The chart above reflects the most commonly used gauges and hook sizes for specific yarn categories.

CROCHET HOOKS	
U.S.	**Metric mm**
B-1	2.25
C-2	2.75
D-3	3.25
E-4	3.5
F-5	3.75
G-6	4
7	4.5
H-8	5
I-9	5.5
J-10	6
K-10½	6.5
L-11	8
M/N-13	9
N/P-15	10
P/Q	15
Q	16
S	19

GAUGE

Exact gauge is essential for proper size. Before beginning your project, make a sample swatch in the yarn and hook specified. After completing the swatch, measure it, counting your stitches and rows or rounds carefully. If your swatch is larger or smaller than specified, **make another, changing hook size to get the correct gauge.** Keep trying until you find the size hook that will give you the specified gauge.

BASIC	Projects using basic stitches. May include basic increases and decreases.
EASY	Projects may include simple stitch patterns, color work, and/or shaping.
INTERMEDIATE	Projects may include involved stitch patterns, color work, and/or shaping.
COMPLEX	Projects may include complex stitch patterns, color work, and/or shaping using a variety of techniques and stitches simultaneously.

MARKERS

Markers are used to help distinguish the beginning of each round being worked. Place a 2" (5 cm) scrap piece of yarn before the first stitch of each round, moving marker after each round is complete ***(Fig. 1)***.

Fig. 1

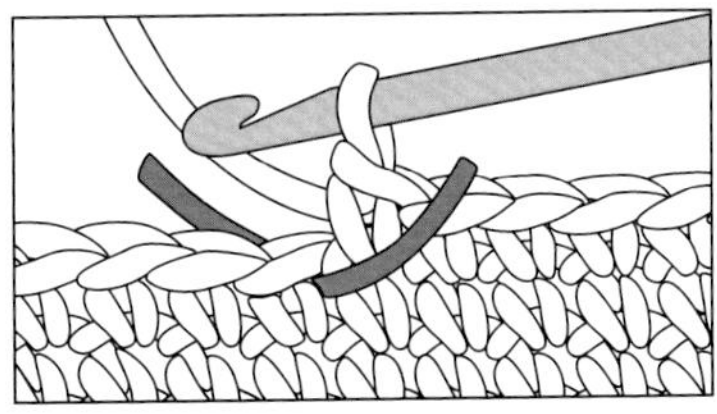

JOINING WITH A SLIP ST

When instructed to join with a slip st, begin with a slip knot on hook. Insert hook in st or sp indicated, YO and draw through st or sp **and** through loop on hook.

Fig. 2

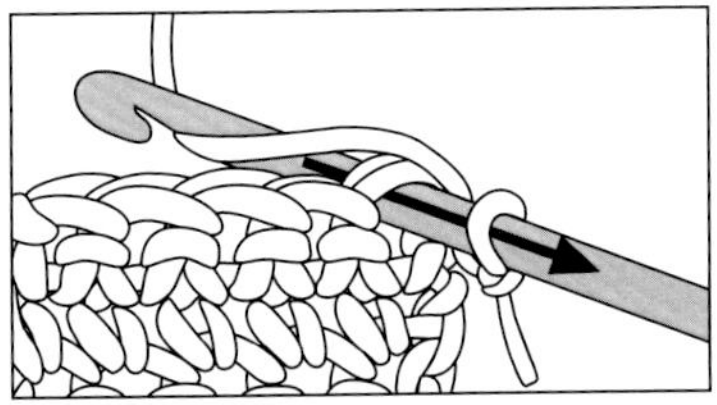

JOINING WITH A SC

Begin with a slip knot on hook. Insert hook in st indicated, YO and pull up a loop, YO and draw through both loops on hook.

Fig. 3

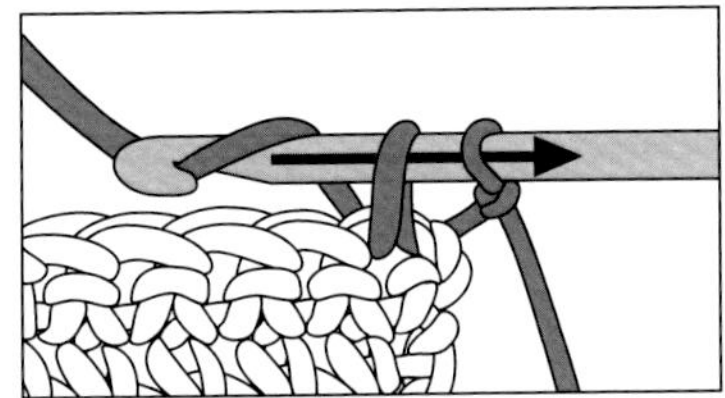

ADJUSTABLE RING

Wind the yarn around two fingers to form a ring ***(Fig. 4a)***.

Fig. 4a

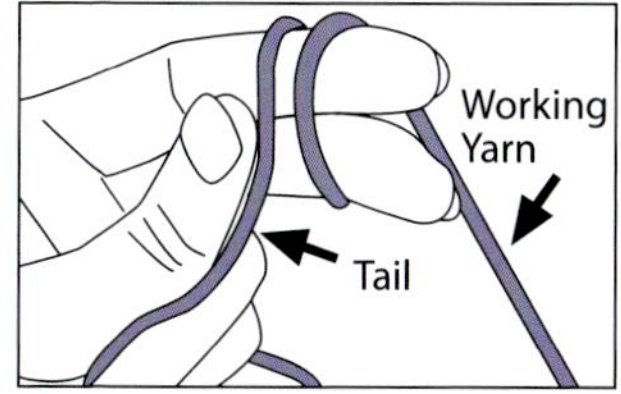

Slide the yarn off your fingers and grasp the strands at the top of the ring ***(Fig. 4b)***.

Fig. 4b

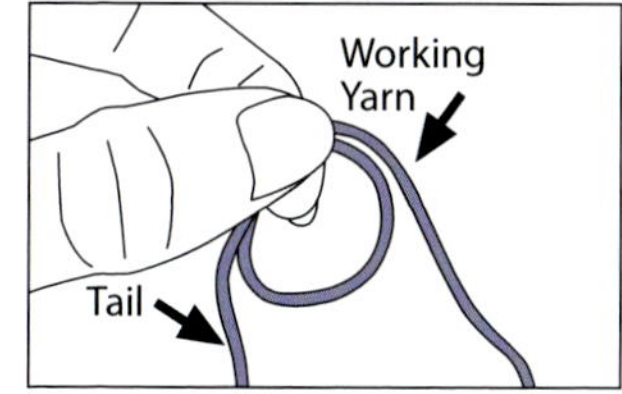

Insert the hook from **front** to **back** into the ring, pull up a loop, YO and draw through the loop on hook to lock the ring ***(Fig. 1c)***.

Fig. 4c

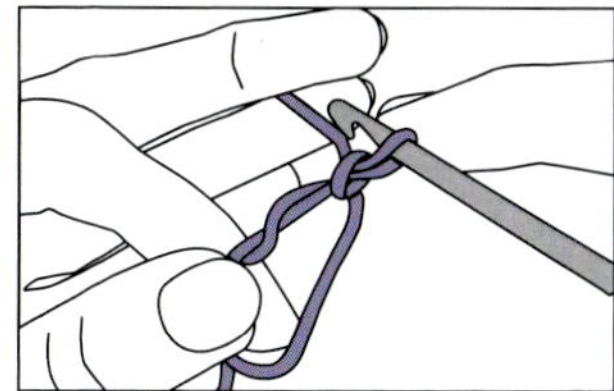

Working around **both** strands, work stitches in the ring as specified, then pull the yarn end to close ***(Fig. 1d)***.

Fig. 4d

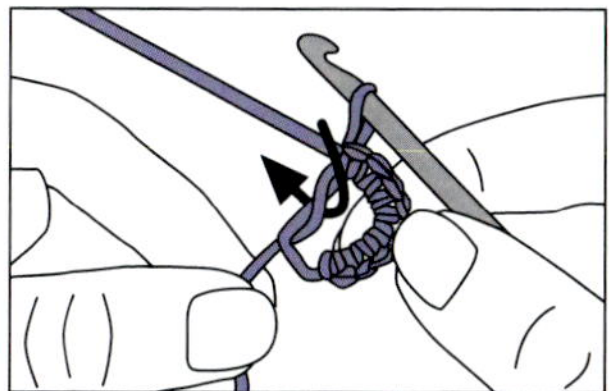

TOP LOOP OF A CHAIN

Work in loops indicated by arrows ***(Fig. 5)***.

Fig. 5

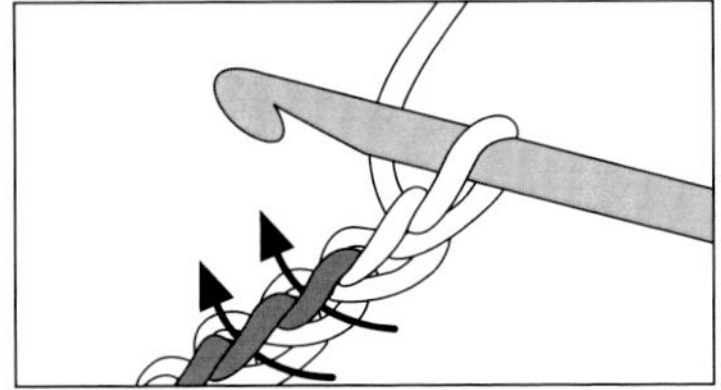

FREE LOOPS OF A CHAIN

Work in loop indicated by arrow ***(Fig. 6)***.

Fig. 6

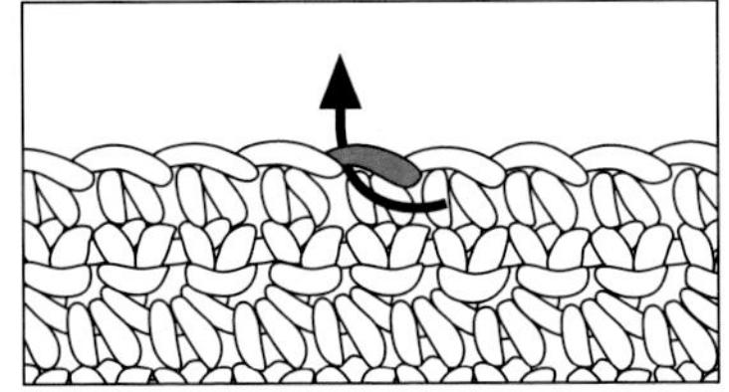

BACK OR FRONT LOOPS ONLY

Work in loop indicated by arrow ***(Fig. 7)***.

Fig. 7

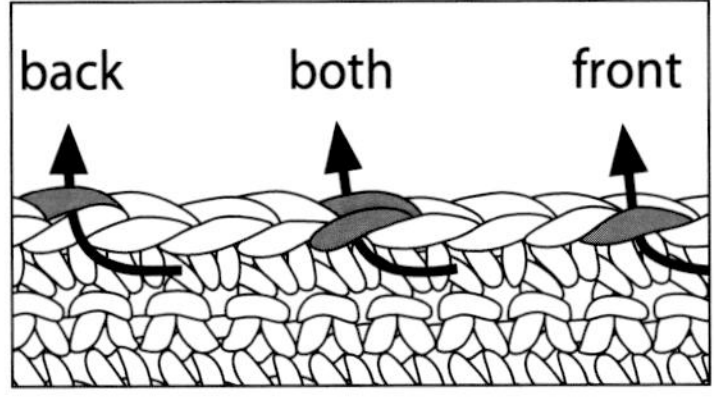

POM-POM

Cut a piece of cardboard 5" (12.5 cm) wide by 3½" (9 cm) tall. Wind the yarn around the cardboard until it is approzimately ¾" (19 mm) thick in the middle ***(Fig. 8a)***.

Fig. 8a

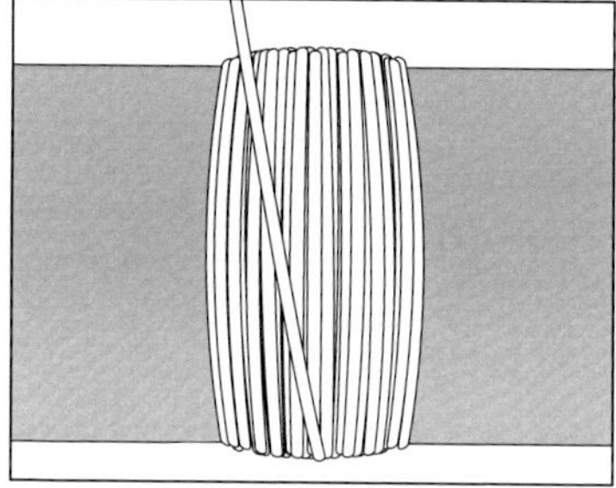

Carefully slip the yarn off the cardboard and tie an 18" (45.5 cm) length of yarn around the middle ***(Fig. 8b)***.

Fig. 8b

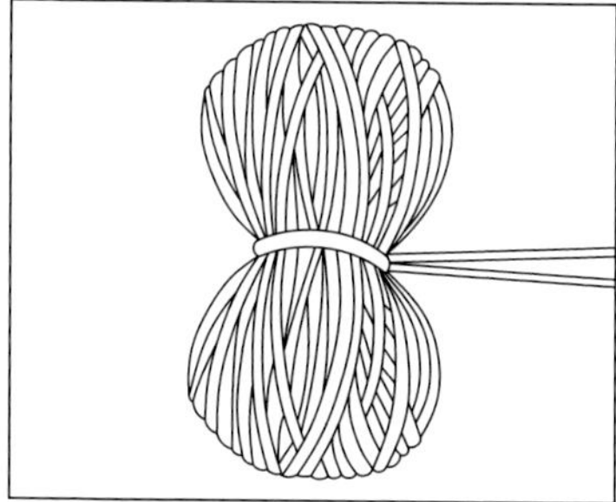

Leave yarn ends long enough to attach the pom-pom. Cut the loops on both ends and tie the pom-pom into a smooth ball ***(Fig. 8c)***.

Fig. 8c

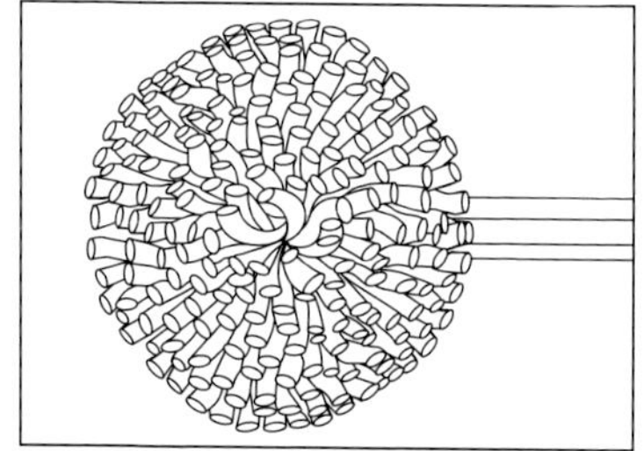

BASIC CROCHET STITCHES

Chain

To work a chain stitch, begin with a slip knot on the hook. Bring the yarn **over** the hook from **back** to **front**, catching the yarn with the hook and turning the hook slightly toward you to keep the yarn from slipping off. Draw the yarn through the slip knot *(Fig. 9)* **(first chain st made,** ***abbreviated ch)***.

Fig. 9

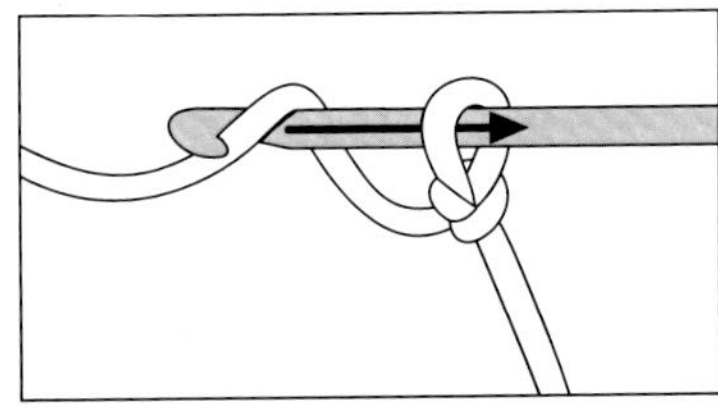

Working Into The Chain

Method 1: Insert hook into the back ridge of each chain *(Fig. 10a)*.

Fig. 10a

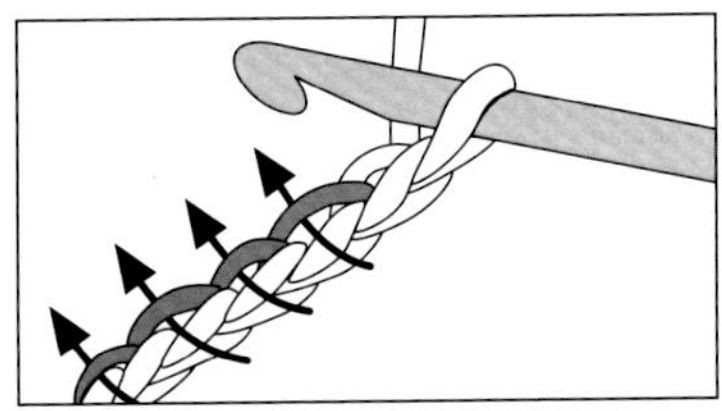

Method 2: Insert hook under the top two strands of each chain *(Fig. 10b)*.

Fig. 10b

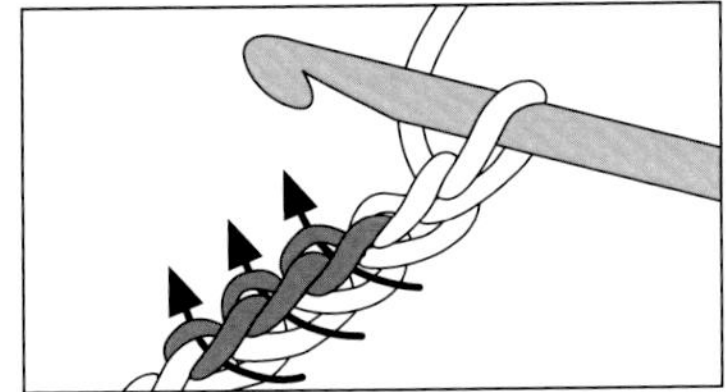

Slip Stitch

To work a slip stitch, insert hook in the stitch indicated, YO and draw through st **and** through the loop on the hook ***(Fig. 11)*** **(slip stitch made, *abbreviated slip st)*.**

Fig. 11

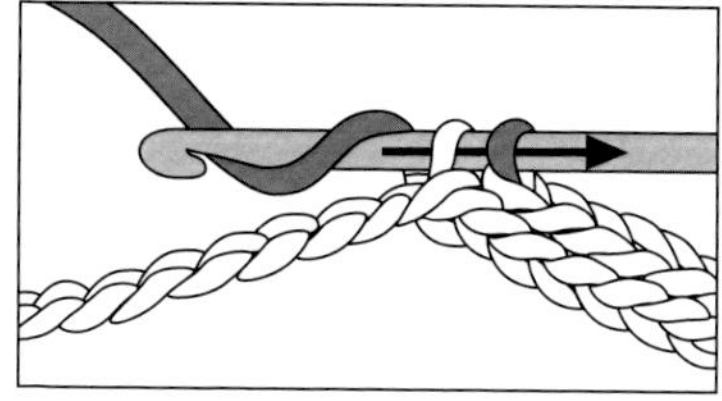

Single Crochet

Insert hook in stitch indicated, YO and pull up a loop, YO and draw through both loops on hook ***(Fig. 12)*** **(single crochet made, *abbreviated sc)*.**

Fig. 12

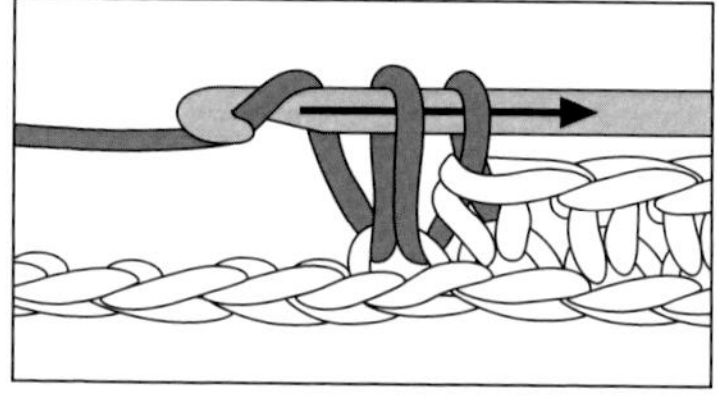

Half Double Crochet

YO, insert hook in stitch indicated, YO and pull up a loop, YO and draw through all 3 loops on hook ***(Fig. 13)*** **(half double crochet made, *abbreviated hdc)*.**

Fig. 13

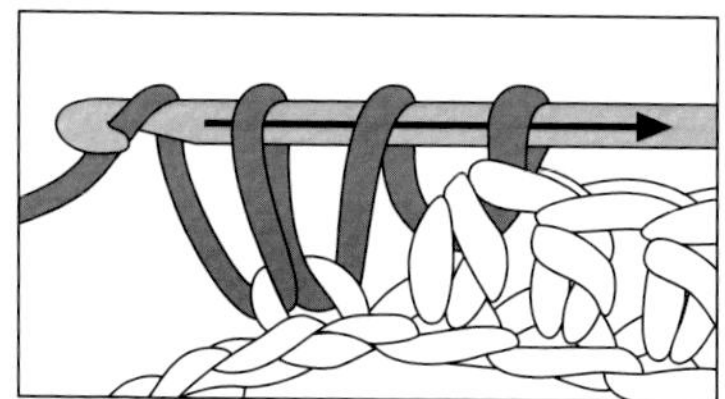

YARN INFORMATION

The projects in this book were made using a Jumbo Weight Yarn. Any brand of jumbo weight yarn may be used. It is best to refer to the yardages/meters when determining how many balls or skeins to purchase. Remember, to achieve the same look, it is the weight of the yarn that is important, not the brand.

We have made every effort to ensure that these instructions are accurate and complete. we cannot, however, be responsible for human error, typographical mistakes, or variations in individual work.

Copyright © 2024 by Leisure Arts, Inc., 104 Champs Blvd., STE 100, Maumelle, AR 72113-6738, www.leisurearts.com. All rights reserved. This publication is protected under federal copyright laws. Reproduction or distribution of this publication or any other Leisure Arts, publication, including publications which are out of print, is prohibited unless specifically authorized. This includes, but is not limited to, any form of reproduction or distribution on or through the internet, including posting, scanning, or e-mail transmission.

Made in U.S.A.